QUEBEC

RENNAY CRAATS

Weigl

CALGARY

www.weigl.com

Published by Weigl Educational Publishers Limited
6325 – 10 Street SE
Calgary, Alberta, Canada
T2H 2Z9
Web site: http://www.weigl.com
Copyright © 2002 WEIGL EDUCATIONAL PUBLISHERS LIMITED

National Library of Canada Cataloguing in Publication Data
Craats, Rennay, 1973-
 Quebec

 (Eye on Canada)
 Includes Index
 ISBN 1-896990-92-4 (bound) -- ISBN 1-894705-48-3 (pbk.)

 1. Quebec--Juvenile literature. I. Title. II. Series:
FC2911.2.C7318 2001   j971.4   C2001-910486-3
F1052.4.C73 2001

Printed and bound in Canada
1 2 3 4 5 6 7 8 9 0   05 04 03 02 01

Photograph Credits
Every reasonable effort has been made to trace ownership and to obtain
permission to reprint copyright material. The publishers would be pleased to
have any errors or omissions brought to their attention so that they may be
corrected in subsequent printings.

Cover: Corel Corporation; Inside Cover: Gouvernement du Québec; Agence Stock
Photo: pages 3B, 6BL, 6BR, 7MR, 9T, 12TR, 13B, 14TR, 15T, 16T, 16B, 18B, 21B,
22T, 22B, 23BL, 23BR, 24MR, 24B, 25MR; Archives nationales du Québec: page
17B; Barrett & Mackay: pages 3M, 4T, 4B, 5M, 7TL, 8T, 10BL, 10BR, 20T, 20B;
Bettman/Corbis: pages 26T, 26B, 27T, 27B; Corbis Corporation: page 13T; Corel
Corporation: pages 11T, 11B, 14BR; National Archives of Canada: pages
7B(PA180808), 18T(C9711), 19M(C1078), 19B(C11925); Noranda Inc.: page 9B;
Parks Canada: page 12BL; Photodisc: pages 8MR, 14BL, 15B, 25ML; Rogers
Communications Inc.: pages 3T, 17B.

Project Coordinator
Jill Foran
Design
Warren Clark
Layout
Bryan Pezzi
Cover Design
Terry Paulhus
Photo Researcher
Joe Nelson

CONTENTS

INTRODUCTION

Many of the historic buildings in Quebec City reflect the classical architectural styles found in France.

QUICK FACTS

Quebec has a total land area of 1,540,680 square kilometres. This is larger than the United States's largest state, Alaska.

Quebec makes up more than 15 percent of Canada's total area.

Quebec is nicknamed "La belle province." This means "beautiful province" in English.

Quebec was one of the four provinces that formed Canada on July 1, 1867.

The capital of Quebec is Quebec City. It is located at the mouth of the Saint Lawrence River.

Quebec is by far Canada's largest province in area. It is even larger than many countries in the world—Germany, France, and Spain could all easily fit inside Quebec's borders. Quebec also has the second largest population in the country, after Ontario. Most of Quebec's population speaks French, making it unique among the Canadian provinces.

The French influence can be seen throughout the province. French-style homes line Quebec's streets, and schools preserve the ancestral language by teaching students in French. Street signs are usually in French as well as English. Quebecers honour their French roots with festivals and celebrations throughout the year. They also work hard to preserve and celebrate their heritage.

Quebec is sandwiched between the Atlantic provinces and central Canada. Newfoundland and Labrador border Quebec to the east, and Ontario borders it to the west and south. New Brunswick also borders it to the south, as do the U.S. states of Maine, Vermont, New Hampshire, and New York. Water serves as the border for much of Quebec. Hudson Strait and Ungava Bay are to the north, while Hudson Bay and James Bay are to the west. The waves of the Gulf of Saint Lawrence crash against Quebec's southeastern shores.

Getting to Quebec is easy. The province has three international airports—one in Quebec City and two in Montreal. It also has many landing facilities for seaplanes and helicopters. Many Quebecers live in cities that are close together, so the province does not have a highly developed rail system. Instead, it has rapid transit trains that link the major cities. For travellers who prefer driving, Quebec is crisscrossed with roads and highways that bring people to where they need to be. The province also has about thirty-five ports that host ships from around the world.

Quebec has about 28,000 km of provincial roads and highways. About 70 percent of these are paved.

The Saint Lawrence Seaway is one of the busiest waterways in the world. More than 2 billion tonnes of cargo have been transported via this waterway since it opened in 1959.

Baie-Comeau, Montreal, Sorel, Port-Cartier, and Sept-Îles, are Quebec's major ports.

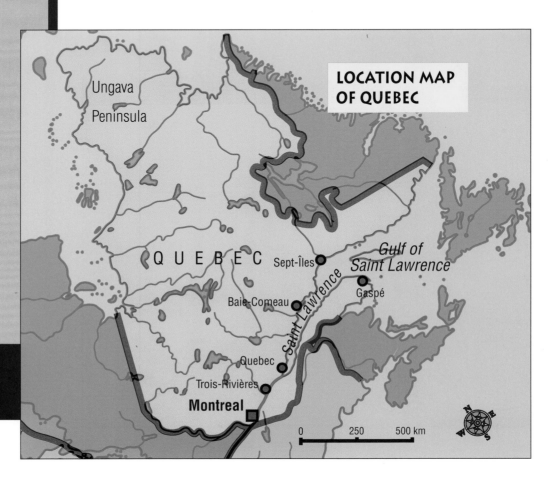

LOCATION MAP OF QUEBEC

Ungava Peninsula

Q U E B E C   Sept-Îles

Gulf of Saint Lawrence

Saint Lawrence

Gaspé

Baie-Comeau

Quebec

Trois-Rivières

Montreal

0   250   500 km

Quebec's varied landscape makes it one of the most beautiful provinces in Canada. The incredible land is home to an abundance of animal and plant life. The province boasts clear rivers and lakes, lush forests, and rugged cliffs. Quebec was once covered with glaciers. These rivers of ice crept along grinding rocks, carving out wide valleys, and transporting soil as they moved. As the glaciers melted, the valleys filled with water to form thousands of sparkling lakes.

Quebec has three fascinating land regions, including the Saint Lawrence Lowlands, the Appalachian Highlands, and the Canadian Shield. Some of the rocks found in the Shield are among the oldest in the world.

Quebec's sparkling lakes and rivers provide excellent opportunities for outdoor recreation.

QUICK FACTS

The Canadian Shield is too cold for most crops. It is, however, rich in natural resources.

The provincial motto is "Je me souviens." In English, this means "I remember."

Across the Ungava Bay and the Hudson Strait lies Nunavut, Canada's newest territory.

Quebec's flag is the *fleurdelisé*. It has a white cross on a blue background and a white *fleur-de-lis* flower in each corner.

Quebec received its name from the Algonquin. "Kebek" is an Algonquian word meaning "where the river narrows."

Quebec has produced many important political figures throughout its history. In 1896, Sir Wilfred Laurier became the first French Canadian to serve as Canada's prime minister. He held the longest unbroken term as prime minister in Canadian history. Brian Mulroney was another Quebecer to serve as prime minister. He won the biggest parliamentary victory ever, in the general election in 1984. Quebecer Jean Chrétien is from Shawinigan. He was the first French Canadian minister of Finance in 1977, and became Attorney General in 1980, and the opposition leader in 1990. In 1993, Chrétien became prime minister.

Quebec City is the only walled city in North America. It is also one of the few cities in the world that has been designated as a World Heritage Site.

Louis St. Laurent's mother was English, and his father was French. This gave him a unique perspective on the country when he served as prime minister from 1948 until 1957.

Perhaps the most notable leader from Quebec was Pierre Trudeau. People adored this **charismatic** man. He was known for encouraging trade and for establishing constitutional independence from Great Britain in 1982. Trudeau retired in 1984. When he died in 2000, the country mourned the loss of a legend.

"Trudeaumania" swept the country during Canada's 1968 election. Thousands of people attended Trudeau's rallies.

Prime Minister Jean Chrétien believes in keeping Quebec a part of Canada.

LAND AND CLIMATE

The Saint Lawrence Lowlands Region is the most fertile and most developed of Quebec's three land regions.

Quebec is made up of three land regions. The Canadian Shield covers more than 90 percent of the province. The Shield is characterized by many lakes and small hills, and neither people nor plants thrive in the harsh northern parts. The Appalachian Highlands are to the south of the Saint Lawrence River. The highlands run from the Gaspé Peninsula south to Alabama in the United States. This region has many **plateaus** and valleys. The Saint Lawrence Lowlands Region falls between the other two regions. It consists of Anticosti Island and the low-lying land of the Saint Lawrence River Valley. It is the heart of Quebec's successful farming industry.

Quebec's climate is greatly affected by wind. Winds from the North Pole sweep down across Quebec and over the most populated areas of the province. Heavy rain and snow falls where these cold winds meet the warmer air from the south. Unpredictable temperatures and long, cold winters are the result. Summers are often hot. Southern Quebec is humid, with about 1,000 millimetres of precipitation each year. Areas further north experience colder and drier weather.

QUICK FACTS

Quebec's highest point is Mont D'Iberville, at 1,652 metres.

There are many lakes and rivers in the province. The most important waterway is the Saint Lawrence River. It is 3,700 km long and flows into the Gulf of Saint Lawrence.

Îles de la Madeleine (Magdalen Islands), Anticosti Island, and Île d'Orléans are all part of Quebec.

The coldest temperature ever recorded in Quebec is –54° Celsius. The highest is 40°C.

In northern Quebec, winters are long, and ice and snow often last past June.

The Montmorency Falls, near Quebec City, are 83 m high. Roughly 35,000 litres of water flow over the falls every second. In the winter, the water freezes into a huge ice cone known as the "sugar loaf."

NATURAL RESOURCES

Quebec is rich in natural resources. It ranks third in Canada in non-fuel materials. Many resources and minerals are **refined** in Quebec, even if they were not mined there. Bauxite, which is a source of aluminum, is imported and refined. Zinc, iron ore, and copper are important natural resources mined and refined in the province. Copper is mined at Murdocville and refined in Rouyn-Noranda, which has one of the largest custom copper **smelters** in the world. Iron ore is mined along the Quebec-Labrador border. These mines provide nearly half the country's supply of iron ore. There are also gold mines around Rouyn-Noranda and Val-d'Or.

Trees are another important natural resource in the province. Quebec has more forest than any other province in the country. Much of this land is owned by the provincial government. Some trees are used to make wood for construction, while others are used to produce maple syrup. Quebec's trees not only provide a boost to the economy, they also draw in tourists who want to enjoy the beauty of the province's forests.

The copper smelter in Rouyn–Noranda was built in 1922. It now employs over 800 people and processes over 300,000 tonnes of copper per year.

Quebec is the leading producer of maple syrup in the country. About 40 litres of tree sap is needed to make I litre of maple syrup.

The area northwest of Montreal is rich in minerals such as magnesite, molybdenum, kaolin, graphite, and silica.

The Ungava Bay has become a leading nickel-copper-cobalt mining area.

Quebec makes more aluminum than any other province.

Quebec is the world's leading producer of asbestos.

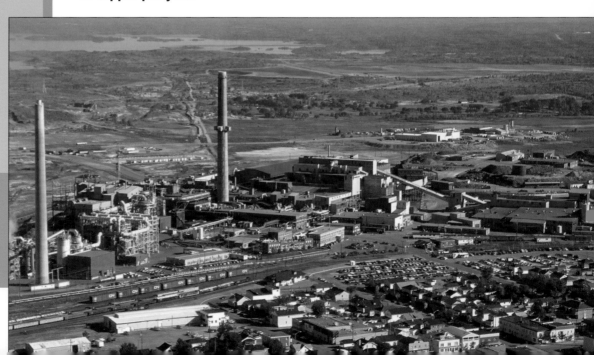

PLANTS AND ANIMALS

QUICK FACTS

More than two-thirds of Quebec is covered with forests. Most of these are **boreal** forests with **coniferous** trees, such as balsam fir, black spruce, hemlock, and jack pine. Quebec's **temperate forests** lie south of the boreal forests. The **deciduous** trees in the temperate forests are mostly sugar maple, birch, elm, and oak. Parts of Quebec do not support much plant life at all. The extreme north is an area of **tundra**. This frozen land is home mainly to mosses, lichens, and low shrubs.

In the spring and summer, many of Quebec's forests are carpeted with wildflowers, including bellworts, bloodroots, dogtooth violets, trilliums, and spring beauties. Blue irises, goldenrods, and milkweed bloom throughout the province, while buttercups, daisies, prairie strawberries, and raspberries are found in Quebec's prairie lands.

Quebec's boreal forests cover a large portion of the Canadian Shield region.

Over 250 bird species can be seen at the Cap-Tourmente National Wildlife Area, east of Beaupré.

More than 2,500 kinds of flowers grow in Quebec. This number is so high because of the vastly different habitats found in the province.

Over 25,000 different plant species can be found at Montreal's Botanical Gardens. These botanical gardens are the third largest in the world.

Quebec's provincial flower is the white lily. It does not grow naturally in Canada, but was chosen because it resembles the fleur-de-lis.

Every year, thousands of caribou migrate between their summer feeding grounds and their winter forest homes.

Wolves are no longer found in southern Quebec. Coyotes have taken over the area, and the wolves have moved further north.

There are about 500 beluga whales living near Quebec's shores.

Quebecers love to bird-watch. The province has more than 100 bird-watching clubs. Many people also have bird feeders at their homes, creating a successful birdseed industry.

The snowy owl has been Quebec's provincial bird since 1897.

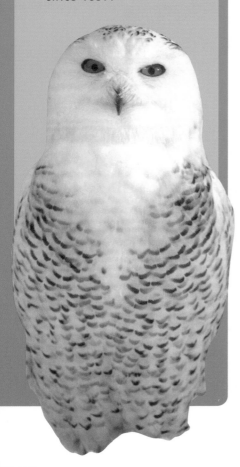

From polar bears to beavers, Quebec is home to a wide variety of animal life. Large animals such as caribou, deer, black bears, and moose all live in Quebec's forests. Smaller animals in the province include skunks, raccoons, foxes, and squirrels.

A variety of birds are also found in Quebec. Some live in the province all year round. Snowy owls, chickadees, and sparrows are all permanent residents. The hermit thrush, ruffed grouse, Canada jay, and woodpecker are all found in Quebec's forests. Many other birds come to Quebec for the summer, then fly south for the winter.

The waters surrounding Quebec support a great deal of animal life. Whale-watchers keep their eyes on the Gulf of Saint Lawrence for signs of the beluga and blue whales. Many different kinds of seals can also be spotted. The rivers and streams are full of fish, from northern pike and muskellunge to bass and trout. Atlantic salmon are abundant in the Saint Lawrence River's **tributaries**. Cod, mackerel, snow crab, shrimp, and lobster are all fished and harvested in the Gulf.

TOURISM

About 22 million tourists travel to Quebec each year to visit its historical landmarks and to experience its breathtaking scenery. Quebec City's cobblestone streets and old-French flair draw visitors from all over the world. Montreal also offers tourists historic attractions, as well as beautiful parks and unbeatable shopping. Many tourists visit the province to take advantage of the countless activities its lakes, rivers, and mountains have to offer.

History lovers have many attractions to choose from in Quebec. The Battle of Châteauguay National Historic Park holds re-enactments depicting the lives of the troops who fought during the War of 1812. Visitors to Fort Lennox National Historic Park, on Île-aux-Noix, can explore one of the largest forts in the country. The Citadel, in Quebec City, is also a popular attraction. It is the largest fort in North America still used as a military base. This star-shaped fortress was built in the late 1800s and has twenty-five buildings for tourists to see. It also has a museum that traces the province's long military history.

The Battle of Châteauguay historic site commemorates the history of the only battle to take place in Quebec during the War of 1812.

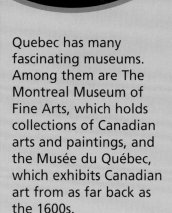

Quebec has many fascinating museums. Among them are The Montreal Museum of Fine Arts, which holds collections of Canadian arts and paintings, and the Musée du Québec, which exhibits Canadian art from as far back as the 1600s.

The Canadian Museum of Civilization is located in Hull. This museum has over 4 million artifacts relating to Canada's fascinating social history.

The Chateau Frontenac is Quebec City's best known landmark. Since its opening in 1893, thousands of visitors have stayed in its 600 luxurious rooms.

INDUSTRY

Quebec's aerospace industry generates more than $8 billion for the province's economy and employs about 40,000 people.

There are about 10,000 factories, mills, and refineries in Quebec.

The pulp and paper industry is important in Quebec. The province provides about one-third of all the pulp and paper produced in Canada.

Most of Quebec's aerospace industries are based in Montreal.

Marc Garneau, from Quebec City, was the first Canadian astronaut to enter space. He flew on the space shuttle *Challenger* twice—in 1984 and 1996.

Quebec is home to some of the largest hydroelectric power plants in the world.

With all of the water around Quebec, it is no wonder that fishing is a major industry. There are about forty fish-processing plants in Quebec. These plants provide fish lovers around the country with fresh, salted, smoked, and canned fish.

Water is also important to other Quebec industries. **Hydroelectric** power has become incredibly profitable in Quebec. This form of power supplies about 95 percent of the province's electricity. The enormous water reserves in the province make it relatively inexpensive for Quebec to generate hydroelectricity. Excess power is exported to the rest of Canada and to the United States. Quebec has become the leading producer of hydroelectricity in North America.

Nearly half of Canada's aerospace industry is located in Quebec. It is the fifth-largest aerospace centre in the world. This industry produces airplanes, hydraulics, and **avionics**. Many of Quebec's successful aerospace companies are taking their expertise a step further in the satellite technology field.

GOODS AND SERVICES

Quebec produces many different agricultural products. Dairy products are among the most important—Quebec has the largest dairy industry in the country. Quebec dairy farmers produce delicious cheese, ice cream, milk, and butter. Most dairy cattle are raised in the Saint Lawrence Lowlands. This area has fertile soil that is ideal for grazing cattle and growing crops. Some farmers raise livestock. Pigs, beef cattle, sheep, and chickens are the most common livestock in Quebec. Other farmers grow crops, including corn, wheat, barley, oat, and soybean crops. Farmers also grow vegetables and fruits, such as potatoes, peas, lettuce, carrots, blueberries, and apples.

Manufacturing employs about 19 percent of Quebec's workers. Most of the large factories can be found around Montreal. Food-processing plants throughout the province make pasta, butter, cheese, and soft drinks. Large bakeries and meat-packing plants are found in Montreal.

Quebec's commercial bakeries are a significant sector of the province's food-processing industry.

QUICK FACTS

There are about 40,000 farms in Quebec, mostly along the Saint Lawrence River.

About 85 percent of Quebec's international exports go to the United States.

Quebec raises more chickens and eggs than any other province except Ontario.

McGill University was founded in Montreal in 1821. It is Canada's oldest university.

Montreal is one of Canada's leading financial centres. It hosts a major stock exchange.

Many of the largest engineering research companies in the world are based in Montreal.

Canada's first radio broadcast was made in Montreal in 1919. Today, the province has about 135 radio stations and thirty television stations.

About 200 magazines and 250 newspapers are published in Quebec. Eleven of these papers are published daily, and ten are in French.

It is illegal for residents in Quebec to have personalized license plates.

Students at the University of Montreal can take courses in a wide variety of subjects. The school has over 250 undergraduate programs.

Chemicals are important manufactured products in Quebec. Industrial chemicals, toiletries, and **pharmaceuticals** are among the province's top chemical products. Quebec is a vital centre for pharmaceutical research and development in Canada. The province takes on about half of the country's production in this area. Many pharmaceutical jobs in research focus on **biotechnology**.

Information technology is a growing field in Quebec. Telecommunications equipment, electronics, and computer parts are produced in the province. More than 7,000 companies in this field operate in Quebec. This brings billions of dollars to the provincial economy and employs 100,000 Quebecers.

The service industry is an important sector of Quebec's economy. Service employees do not create a product. Instead, they provide services for other people. These services include waiting on tables, taking reservations at a hotel, providing medical care, or selling goods at a store. Many people also work at one of the province's educational institutions, including its five largest universities—the University of Quebec, Laval University, the University of Montreal, McGill University, and Concordia University.

FIRST NATIONS

Three main Native groups—the Algonquians, the Iroquoians, and the Inuit—lived in the Quebec area long before European explorers arrived. There were several groups in the Algonquian nation. Among them were the Algonquin, Attikamek, and Mi'kmaq. The Algonquin and Attikamek made their homes west of the Saint-Maurice River, while the Mi'kmaq lived on the Gaspé Peninsula. Many Native groups in Quebec hunted caribou and elk for food.

The Iroquoians lived mainly in the Saint Lawrence region. The good soil allowed them to farm. Crops supplied most of their food, making it easier for them to settle in one area. They built villages with permanent houses. Many of their longhouses were surrounded by **palisades** with fields of squash, corn, and beans growing outside them.

The Inuit lived in the north along Hudson Bay and the Ungava Peninsula. They relied on seals, whales, caribou, bears, fish, and birds for food, clothing, and shelter.

QUICK FACTS

Many early Inuit used dog power to get around. Dogsleds are still an important method of land transportation for Inuit today.

The Naskapi were hunters who lived in the east. The members of this group who lived further south were called Montagnais, or mountaineers, by the French.

Iroquois women often planted, weeded, and harvested the fields. Men fished, hunted, and traded goods with other groups.

Many Inuit preserve their culture and traditions by continuing their ancestors' methods of hunting and fishing. The Inuit pictured here are enjoying fresh seal meat.

EXPLORERS

When Jacques Cartier reached Canada he thought he had found gold and diamonds. However, when he brought his riches home to France, he was told his gold was worthless iron pyrite, or "fools gold," and his diamonds were quartz.

Explorers traded guns, trinkets, kettles, and blankets with Native Peoples in exchange for furs.

Samuel de Champlain did not come to Canada alone. He brought reformed Franciscan missionaries with him. These Jesuits spent a century trying to convert people to their religion.

European explorers arrived in Quebec on their search for a water passage to Asia. In 1534, King Francis I sent explorer Jacques Cartier to claim the northern part of North America for France. He hoped this area would be rich in gold and other metals. Cartier explored Canada's coast and the river he called Saint Lawrence, but he did not find gold. He returned to the area in 1535 and travelled up the Saint Lawrence River to present-day Montreal Island. He then spent the winter in a village that is now called Quebec City.

French fishermen fished along the coast and traded with the Native Peoples they met when they came ashore. The furs they took back to France increased the country's interest in Canada. In the 1580s, France started sending fur-trading expeditions to the Quebec region.

In 1608, another French explorer arrived in Quebec. Samuel de Champlain built a trading post on the Saint Lawrence River. This area was called New France. Initially, few French people settled there. Other European companies were invited to become involved in the fur trade as long as they brought settlers.

Iroquois from the Quebec region acted as interpreters and guides for Jacques Cartier as he explored the Saint Lawrence River.

EARLY SETTLERS

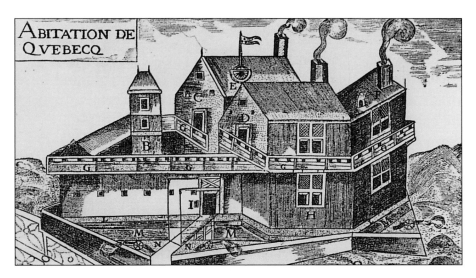

ABITATION DE QVEBECQ

Samuel de Champlain constructed this building in what is now Quebec City. The building housed a number of settlers and served as a storage facility for arms and provisions.

Settlement in New France came about slowly. In the 1620s, interest in fur trading was increasing. By 1628, a fur-trading company called the Company of New France planned to send about 400 settlers to the area. However, a war broke out between France and Britain, preventing many new settlers from moving to the region. Frequent battles for control of the North American colonies continued between France and Britain throughout the late seventeenth and the eighteenth centuries.

Between 1635 and 1663, the population of Quebec's settlements began to grow. Schools and hospitals were built, and the colonies expanded. However, frequent attacks by the Iroquois had settlers in constant fear for their safety. Both the settlers and the fur-trading businesses were in danger. This prompted the French government to act. King Louis XIV began a new push to colonize the area. The king sent French troops to New France to defend against Iroquois attacks. In 1666, the troops invaded Iroquois settlements, burning crops and villages as they advanced. The Iroquois agreed to sign a peace treaty the next year.

QUICK FACTS

New France had only 100 residents in 1627. Fewer than a dozen were women. By 1663, the population had increased to 2,500.

In 1642, a group of missionaries established Montreal as a missionary settlement. While few settlers were eager to move to the settlement, it was an important fur-trading post.

The Company of New France had promised to establish a strong settler community in return for control of fur trading in the area. They did not live up to their end of the bargain. As a result, King Louis XIV dissolved the company.

By 1665, there were 1,300 French soldiers in New France.

Early settlers and Native Peoples had to fight against new diseases and illnesses in the 1750s. The hospitals were full with smallpox patients. Hundreds of people died from the disease.

On September 13, 1759, a monumental battle took place between the French and the British on the Plains of Abraham, outside Quebec City. After only 15 minutes, British General James Wolfe and his 8,500 troops defeated French General Louis-Joseph Montcalm and his 3,000 soldiers and 12,000 armed citizens. Both Wolfe and Montcalm were killed in the battle.

King Louis XIV then set up a French government in Quebec that was led by Jean Talon. Talon attracted thousands of immigrants to the area, and the population increased to 6,700 by 1672. Soon, farmers were harvesting enough food to feed their colony, with more for exporting or trading. Sawmills, tanneries, breweries, and a shipyard were built to take advantage of Quebec's natural resources. Despite this growth, settlers had many obstacles to overcome as they established their towns. Flooding, cold weather, crop failure, and supply ships intercepted by the British created many hardships. Hundreds of people were poor and hungry, and many had to work hard just to survive.

French settlers also had to survive the transfer of power from France to Britain. In 1760, after countless battles between the two nations, France was defeated. Under the 1763 Treaty of Utrecht, it surrendered almost all of its North American land to Britain. Many settlers resented British rule and were concerned that their French traditions would be threatened. Britain allowed them to have their own laws and their own systems of government in hopes that Quebec would be loyal. After many more wars and conflicts, Quebec's independence continued to develop.

Jean Talon was well respected among the province's early settlers, and New France flourished under his leadership.

POPULATION

More than 7 million people live in Quebec. The majority of the population lives in the southern part of the province. In fact, more than 80 percent of Quebec's population lives in an area that is 320 km long and 97 km wide, making it one of the highest concentrations of people in the country. Montreal and its surrounding areas are home to nearly half of the province's population. Quebec's other metropolitan areas include Chicoutimi-Jonquiere, Ottawa-Hull, Quebec City, and Trois-Rivieres.

Most of the people in Quebec have French ancestry. French Canadians make up about 80 percent of the population. People of British descent make up about 10 percent of Quebec's population. The remaining 10 percent is made up of many Native Peoples, as well as other ethnic groups.

QUICK FACTS

Among Quebec's other major cities are Laval, Longueuil, Gatineau, and Hull.

The Gaspé Peninsula is the least populated region of Quebec.

Until the 1940s, most of Quebec's population was rural. Now, less than one-quarter of Quebecers live in rural areas.

About 88 percent of Quebecers are Roman Catholics.

There are more than 50,000 Native Peoples in Quebec.

Montreal is by far Quebec's largest and busiest city. More than 3 million people live in the Montreal metropolitan area.

Canadian women could vote in federal elections by 1918, and most could vote in provincial matters by 1925. Thérèse Casgain successfully led Quebec women in demanding the right to vote in provincial elections in 1940.

Highly populated areas of Quebec are split into ninety-five regional municipalities. These are run by councils made up of elected mayors and alderpeople.

Quebec has seventy-five representatives in the Federal House of Commons and twenty-four members in the Senate.

POLITICS AND GOVERNMENT

Quebec is governed by a 125-member National Assembly. The members are elected from wards throughout the province and serve five-year terms. The premier of Quebec is the head of the provincial government. The leader of the majority party is usually named premier. He or she has a council of ministers from the members of legislature. These ministers run about twenty departments of government.

Quebec has a different system of laws than the rest of Canada. It follows a system of civil law modelled after French civil code rather than English common law. In common law, cases are decided according to previous decisions. Quebec's judges decide according to rules of the civil code—they can disregard other decisions in similar cases.

Quebec's National Assembly has been meeting at Quebec City's Parliament Building for over 100 years.

CULTURAL GROUPS

On June 24, French Quebecers celebrate Saint-Jean Baptiste Day. This celebration honours Saint John the Baptist, the patron saint of French Canadians.

Many Native groups make their homes in Quebec. Among the various groups are the Inuit, the Algonquian, and the Iroquoian. Many of these peoples live in one of over fifty reservations throughout the province. They work to preserve and share their heritage and culture through traditional art, dancing, and ceremonies.

The largest cultural group in Quebec is the French. When the British controlled the colony's economy and government, Quebec's French people, called Québécois, maintained their own cultures and traditions. The community continues to preserve its culture. Some people in Quebec believe the province should be its own country. They want Quebec to separate from Canada because they feel their unique cultural heritage could be best preserved outside the country.

QUICK FACTS

Many French Canadians are descendants of the original French settlers of the 1600s and 1700s.

Montreal is the second largest French-speaking city in the world. The largest is Paris, France.

French Canadians celebrate their heritage through traditional songs and dances. They host corn-husking parties in the fall, taffy-pulling parties in the winter, and sugaring-off outings in the spring.

About 7,500 Inuit live in villages along the coasts of the Ungava Bay and Hudson Bay.

Since the early 1900s many thousands of people have immigrated to Canada. People from Greece, Portugal, Germany, Hungary, and Armenia came to Quebec in search of a new life. Many immigrants from Asia and Latin America, as well as Caribbean countries including Haiti, also chose to live in Quebec. A large number of Italian and Jewish people have also made their homes in Quebec—mostly in Montreal. These ethnic communities have grown rapidly since the 1950s.

Many of Quebec's ethnic groups have created their own neighbourhoods. Often the styles of their homes and gardens, and their shops and restaurants incorporate aspects of their homelands. Chinatown grew in Montreal after the railway was established in the 1860s. The construction of the railway employed many Chinese labourers. Today, Chinatown is a fascinating part of the city.

Since the end of World War II, about 1 million people from more than eighty countries have become Quebecers.

European immigration brought people from England, Scotland, Ireland, and Italy to Quebec. **Loyalists** also moved to the province to escape the American Revolution.

The Summer Festival in Quebec City showcases African, French, and Quebec musicians.

There are more than 250,000 Italians living in Quebec. They are the province's second largest cultural group.

Quebec's Jewish culture can be experienced at one of the many delicatessens, restaurants, or **synagogues** that are found in Montreal.

Montreal's Chinatown offers the tastes and sights of Chinese culture through its many stores and businesses.

ARTS AND ENTERTAINMENT

Quebecers like to entertain and be entertained. The province hosts nearly 300 festivals and carnivals every year. One of the most famous is the Winter Carnival in Quebec City. This annual event celebrates the season with the help of a snowman called Le Bonhomme Carnaval. For ten days, Quebecers enjoy parades, ice sculptures, and ice skating. To keep Montrealers laughing, the city hosts the largest comedy festival in the world. Just for Laughs International Comedy Festival features talented comedians from around the world and draws about 500,000 spectators to the city each year.

Quebec has produced many successful novelists. One of the province's best-known writers is Mordecai Richler. Much of his writing shows life as a Jewish Canadian in Montreal. His work for young readers, including his *Jacob Two-Two* books, have become must-read books for Canadian children from coast to coast.

Mordecai Richler is one of Canada's most respected authors. He has worked as a novelist, a journalist, and a screenwriter.

QUICK FACTS

Playwright Michel Tremblay had a major impact on Quebec theatre in 1968. His characters talked in street French rather than formal French. His plays have been translated and performed all over the world.

Montrealer Leonard Cohen is a poet and novelist, but he is best known for his songs. In 1991, he was inducted into the Juno Awards Hall of Fame.

Anne Hébert was a Quebec poet and novelist who became famous for her novel *Kamouraska*. Her books were translated and enjoyed by English Canadians as well.

Every August, the Montreal World Film Festival shows movies from about sixty different countries.

The board game Trivial Pursuit was created by two friends in Montreal in 1980. The idea came to them in about 30 minutes, but they spent months researching the questions.

Les Grands Ballets Canadiens is one of Quebec's major ballet companies. It is dedicated to performing ballets composed and choreographed by Canadians.

Piano player Oscar Peterson has won several Grammy Awards and has become a jazz music legend. He started his career as a Montreal teenager and began recording his music at the age of 20.

All types of music can be heard throughout Quebec. The Quebec Symphony Orchestra has been entertaining listeners for nearly 100 years. Montreal's two orchestras are known for their incredible recordings and highly regarded conductors. For those who prefer popular music, Quebec is home to many talented pop stars. Corey Hart and Mitsou rose to fame in the 1980s. Kashtin is a duo consisting of Claude McKenzie and Florent Vallant. They are popular for their unique style of music—they sing in their native Innu language.

One of Quebec's most celebrated singers is Céline Dion. She was one of the first singers to have incredible success in both English and French markets. This songstress from Charlemagne started singing professionally when she was a young girl. She has won several awards, including Felix, Juno, and Grammy Awards. Dion's beautiful voice was heard with her chart-topping song "My Heart Will Go On" in the blockbuster movie *Titanic*.

Céline Dion grew up in a large family. The youngest of fourteen children, Céline began performing with her siblings at the early age of 5.

SPORTS

Quebec's cold winters provide exciting sporting opportunities. Hockey, skating, snowshoeing, and skiing are all popular ways to spend a day. During the summer, residents can enjoy Quebec's beautiful scenery while swimming, bicycling, hiking, or canoeing. For those who would rather watch sports than participate, Quebec has thrilling action in Major League Baseball, the Canadian Football League, and the National Hockey League.

The Montreal Expos is one of only two Major League Baseball teams in Canada. The Expos have thrilled fans since the team was established in 1968. Jose Vidro, Javier Vazquez, and superstar brothers Vladimir and Wilton Guerrero have all kept fans cheering for the team. Football fans in Quebec cheer for the Montreal Alouettes. The team disbanded in 1987 but made a welcome return to the Canadian Football League in 1997. Alouettes fans look to talented footballers, including Anthony Calvillo, Mike Pringle, and Lester Smith, to carry their team to the championships.

The Montreal Expos play their home games at Montreal's Olympic Stadium.

QUICK FACTS

Gaetan Boucher won his first Canadian championship in speed skating when he was only 14 years old. He won three Olympic medals for Canada in 1984.

Lucile Wheeler was the first Canadian skier to win an Olympic medal. She took home a bronze medal in the downhill event in 1956. She was also the first North American to win a world championship, in both slalom and downhill, in 1958.

Hockey player Guy Lafleur led the Montreal Canadiens to five Stanley Cup victories and played from 1971 to 1991.

Hundreds of Quebec sporting groups organize activities in anything from **spelunking** to water-skiing to horseback riding.

When she was 20 years old, goaltender Manon Rheaume made history. She became the first woman to play in an NHL hockey game. She appeared in an exhibition game with the Tampa Bay Lightning.

In 1995, the Quebec Nordiques hockey team was sold and became the Colorado Avalanche.

Jacques Villeneuve's father, Gilles, was known for his daring style of race car driving. He won the Grand Prix six times and died in 1982, when he collided with another car at the Belgian Grand Prix.

Myriam Bédard won two Olympic gold medals in the biathlon in 1994.

Perhaps the most popular professional sport in Quebec is hockey. The Montreal Canadiens have excited fans since 1909. The team boasts more championship wins than any other team in any sport in North America. Through the years, many Canadiens players have become heroes in Quebec. Maurice Richard was a long-time fan favourite through the 1940s, 1950s, and 1960s. His explosive personality and his incredible slapshot earned him the nickname "The Rocket." He scored 544 goals in his career and was the first player to score fifty goals in one season. Jacques Plante was the team's goalie in the 1950s. In 1959, after being cut by a shot, he became the first goalie to insist on wearing a practice mask during games. This idea spread and led to present-day goalies masks. Today's Montreal Canadiens still bring fans out to cheer.

Sports fans who thrive on fast-paced action look to the racetrack. Quebec's Jacques Villeneuve is the province's best-known race car driver. He has won many races including the Indianapolis 500. He also found success driving Formula One cars.

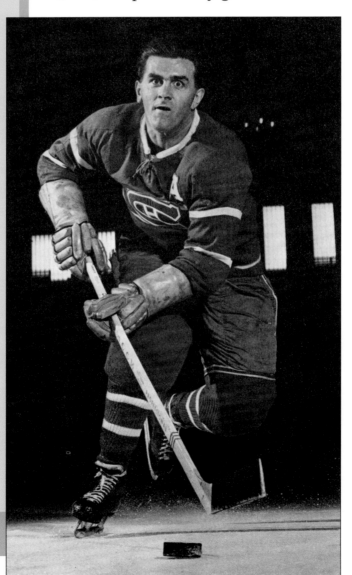

Maurice Richard's incredible skill inspired the creation of a trophy given to the player with the most goals scored in a season. The trophy is named in his honour.

EYE ON CANADA

Quebec is one of the ten provinces and three territories that make up Canada. Compare Quebec's statistics with those of other provinces and territories. What differences and similarities can you find?

Northwest Territories

Entered Confederation:
July 15, 1870

Capital: Yellowknife

Area: 171,918 sq km

Population: 41,606
Rural: 58 percent
Urban: 42 percent

Population Density:
0.24 people per sq km

Yukon

Entered Confederation:
June 13, 1898

Capital: Whitehorse

Area: 483,450 sq km

Population: 30,633
Rural: 40 percent
Urban: 60 percent

Population Density:
0.06 people per sq km

British Columbia

Entered Confederation:
July 20, 1871

Capital: Victoria

Area: 947,800 sq km

Population: 4,023,100
Rural: 18 percent
Urban: 82 percent

Population Density:
4.24 people per sq km

Alberta

Entered Confederation:
September 1, 1905

Capital: Edmonton

Area: 661,190 sq km

Population: 2,964,689
Rural: 20 percent
Urban: 80 percent

Population Density:
4.48 people per sq km

Saskatchewan

Entered Confederation:
September 1, 1905

Capital: Regina

Area: 652,330 sq km

Population: 1,027,780
Rural: 28 percent
Urban: 72 percent

Population Density:
1.57 people per sq km

Manitoba

Entered Confederation:
July 15, 1870

Capital: Winnipeg

Area: 649,950 sq km

Population: 1,143,509
Rural: 28 percent
Urban: 72 percent

Population Density:
1.76 people per sq km

250   500 km

Nunavut

Entered Confederation:
April 1, 1999

Capital: Iqaluit

Area: 1,900,000 sq km

Population: 27,039

Population Density:
0.014 people per sq km

CANADA

Confederation:
July 1,1867

Capital: Ottawa

Area: 9,203,054 sq km

Population: 30,491,294
Rural: 22 percent
Urban: 78 percent

Population Density:
3.06 people
per sq km

Quebec

Entered Confederation:
July 1, 1867

Capital: Quebec City

Area: 1,540,680 sq km

Population: 7,345,390
Rural: 21 percent
Urban: 79 percent

Population Density:
4.77 people per sq km

Newfoundland & Labrador

Entered Confederation:
March 31, 1949

Capital: St. John's

Area: 405,720 sq km

Population: 541,000
Rural: 43 percent
Urban: 57 percent

Population Density:
1.33 people
per sq km

Prince Edward Island

Entered Confederation:
July 1, 1873

Capital:
Charlottetown

Area: 5,660 sq km

Population: 137,980
Rural: 56 percent
Urban: 44 percent

Population Density:
24.38 people
per sq km

Ontario

Entered Confederation:
July 1, 1867

Capital: Toronto

Area: 1,068,580 sq km

Population: 11,513,808
Rural: 17 percent
Urban: 83 percent

Population Density:
10.77 people per sq km

New Brunswick

Entered Confederation:
July 1, 1867

Capital: Fredericton

Area: 73,440 sq km

Population: 754,969
Rural: 51 percent
Urban: 49 percent

Population Density:
10.28 people per sq km

Nova Scotia

Entered Confederation:
July 1, 1867

Capital: Halifax

Area: 55,490 sq km

Population: 939,791
Rural: 45 percent
Urban: 55 percent

Population Density:
16.94 people
per sq km

BRAIN TEASERS

Test your knowledge of Quebec by trying to answer these mind-boggling brain teasers!

1 **True or False:** Parts of Quebec's far north are frozen all year.

2 **Make a Guess:** What disaster occurred in Quebec and Ontario in 1998?

3 **Make a Guess:** What was the Quiet Revolution?

4 **Make a Guess:** Are the Montmorency Falls taller than the Niagara Falls?

5 **Make a Guess:** What were the Meech Lake and Charlottetown Accords?

6 **Make a Guess:** What are Mistassini, Saint-Jean, and Eau Claire?

7 **True or False:** Quebec voted strongly in favour of Confederation in 1867.

8 **True or False:** The biodome is a science training centre.

1. **True.** The Ungava Peninsula is a permafrost area that is frozen to a depth of 275 m. Only the top few centimetres thaw.

2. **A terrible ice storm** hit the region leaving 3 million people without electricity, heat, and water. In some areas, these essentials were not restored for a month.

3. **A time of fast modernization** associated with French-Canadian nationalism. It involved revised hospital insurance and pension plans, an improved education system and labour code, and increased cultural development.

4. **Yes.** They are 84 m high, which is nearly 30 m higher than Niagara Falls.

5. **They were attempts to change** the country's constitution so that it better reflected Quebec and its unique needs.

6. **They are the province's largest lakes.**

7. **False.** A Quebec newspaper printed that the province voted 26 to 21 in favour of joining.

8. **False.** It is a botanical museum that exhibits four ecosystems—tropical forest, polar region, the Saint Lawrence marine environment, and the Laurentian forest.

GLOSSARY

avionics: electronics used in aircraft and rockets

biotechnology: the use of biological processes for industrial purposes

boreal: large area in the northern hemisphere covered mainly in trees including pine, spruce, fir, birch, and poplar

charismatic: a person who charms and inspires great enthusiasm and devotion from others

coniferous: evergreen trees with needles and cones

deciduous: trees or shrubs that shed leaves every year

hydroelectric: energy produced by water power

Loyalists: American colonists who wanted their colonies to remain part of Britain

palisades: fences made with pointed stakes

pharmaceuticals: medicines and prescription drugs

plateaus: level areas of land

refined: a substance that has had impurities or defects removed

smelters: places where ore is melted to obtain metals

spelunking: exploring caves

synagogues: buildings of public worship for those of Jewish faith

temperate forests: mixed and deciduous forests

tributaries: streams that flow into larger bodies of water

tundra: an arctic or subarctic plain with a permanently frozen subsoil

BOOKS

Galvin, Kathryn, *A Quebec Experience*. Edmonton: Arnold Publishing, 1991.

LeVert, Suzanne. *Let's Discover Canada: Quebec*. New York: Chelsea House Publishers, 1991.

Ouellet, Danielle and Jean Provencher. *Discover Canada: Quebec*. Toronto: Grolier Ltd., 1996.

WEB SITES

Tourist Guide
http://www.quebecweb.com/tourisme/introang.html

Montreal Canadiens
http://www.canadiens.com

Travel Quebec
http://www.destinationquebec.com

Some Web sites stay current longer than others. To find information on Quebec, use your Internet search engine to look up such topics as "Montreal," "Quebec City," "Bonhomme," or any other topic you want to research.

INDEX